Beautiful Abandon by Annie Swarm Guldberg

I0419367

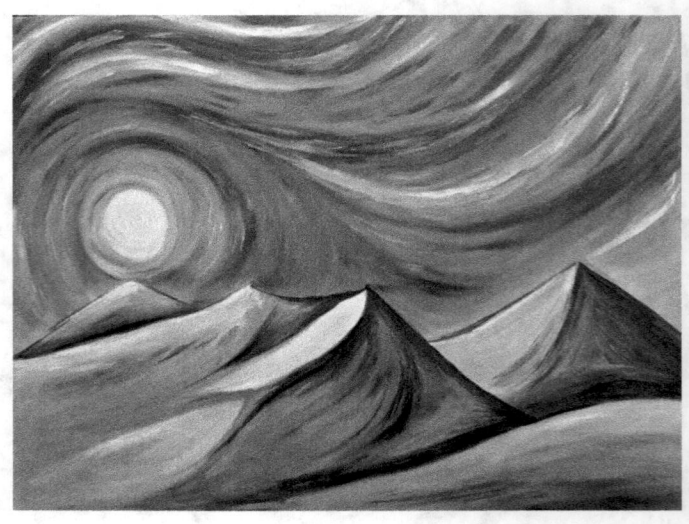

BEAUTIFUL ABANDON BY ANNIE SWARM GULDBERG

Inspired by a photo taken by a friend east of the city of
Abu Dhabi, this painting shows the beauty that
can come from true and complete release.

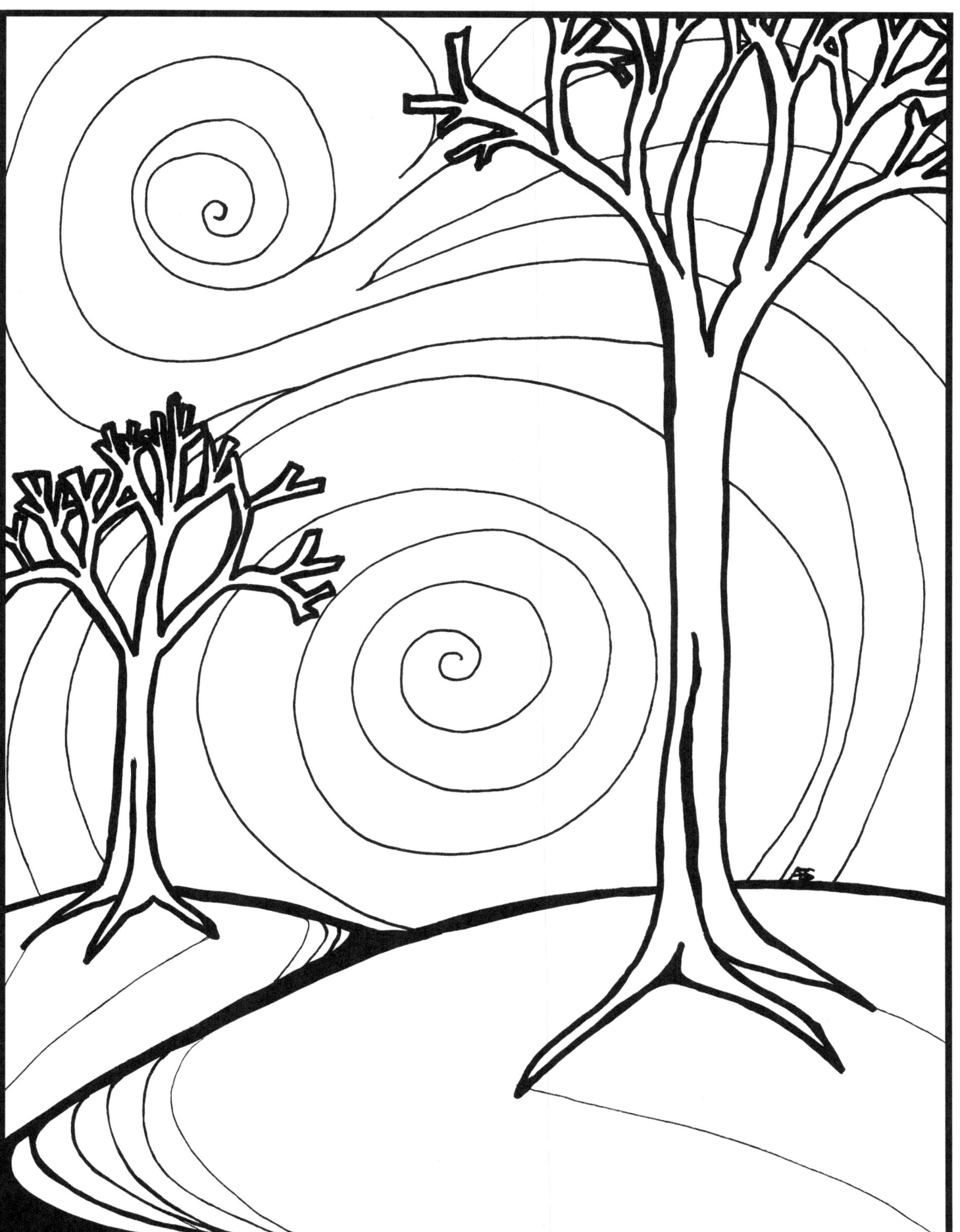

Past, Present, Future by Annie Swarm Guldberg

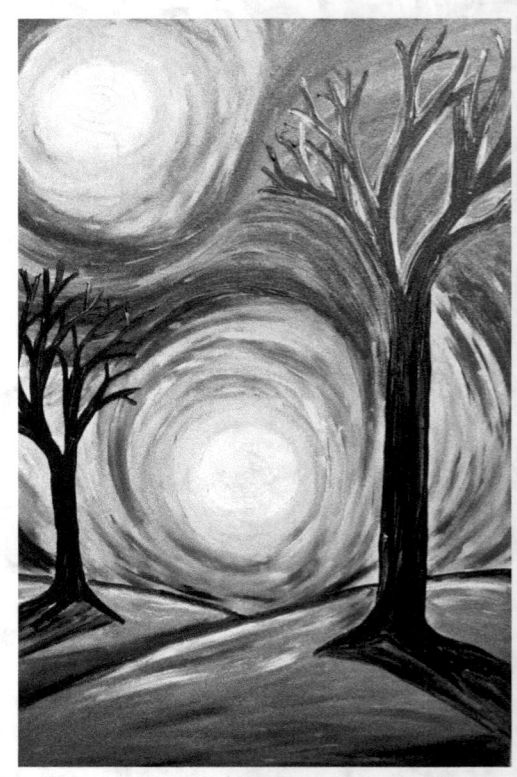

PAST, PRESENT, FUTURE BY ANNIE SWARM GULDBERG

I painted this image on January 1, 2016. I was considering the past (tree in the back), the present (tree in the front) and the exciting future (sky) as I painted. 2016 is the first year I stopped working full time and really considered myself an artist.

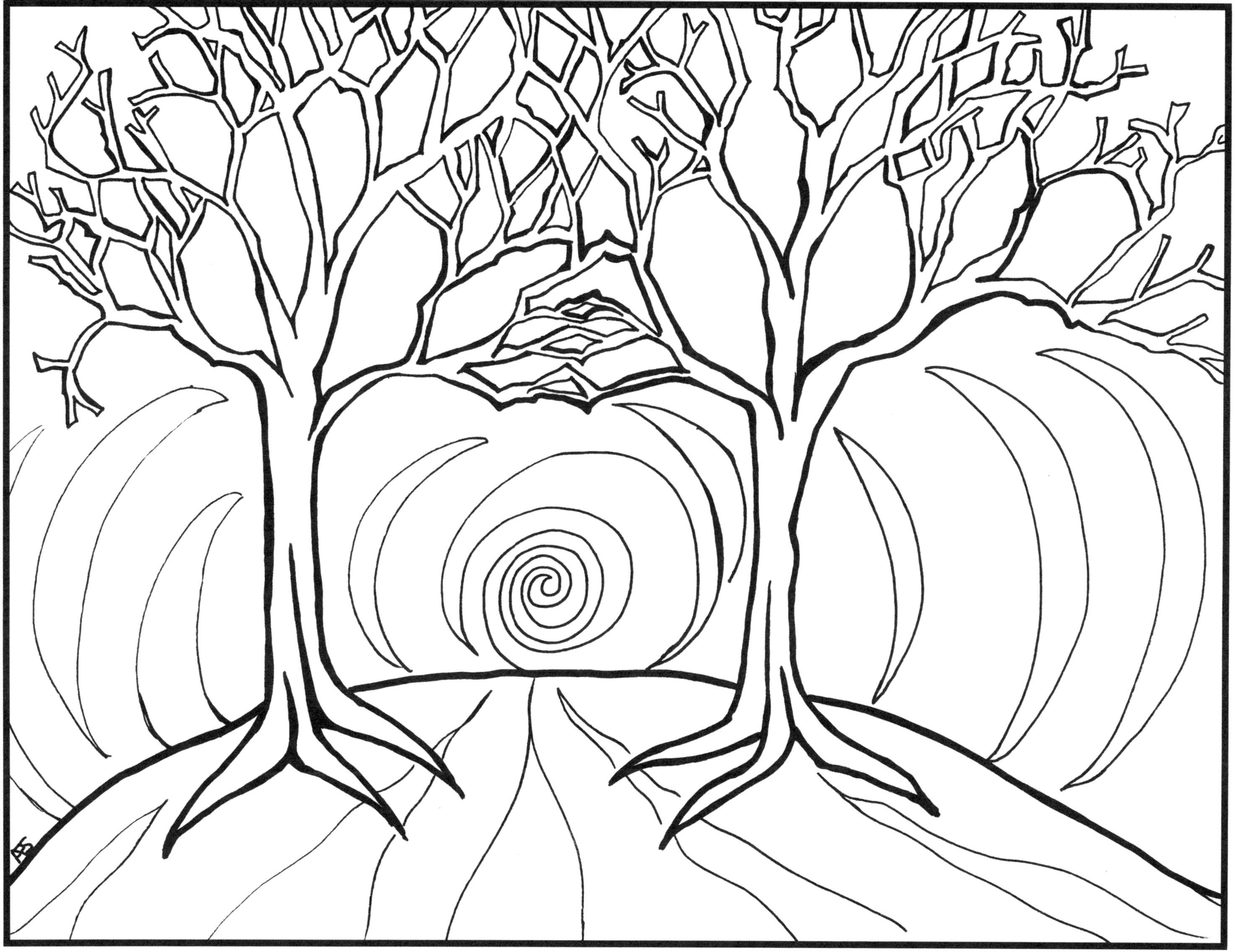

Into The Light by Annie Swarm Guldberg

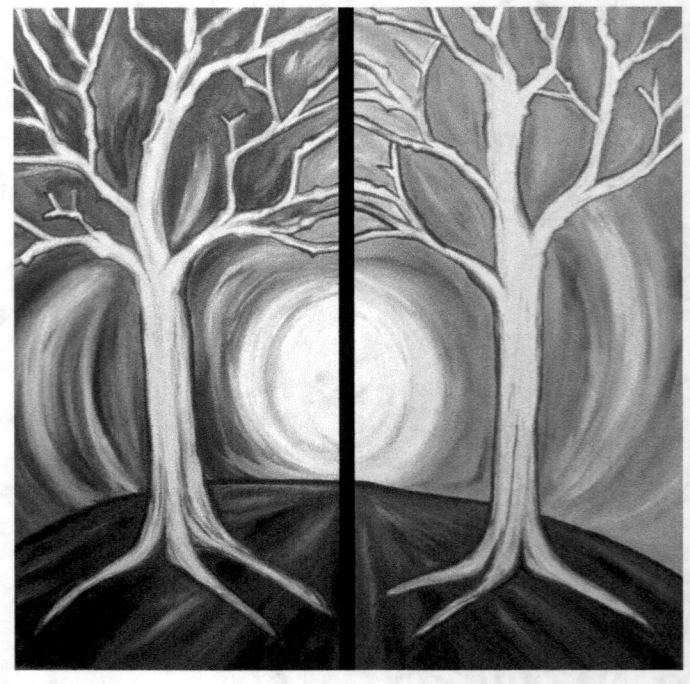

INTO THE LIGHT BY ANNIE SWARM GULDBERG

There is no where to go, but into the light.
Go ahead, see where it leads you.

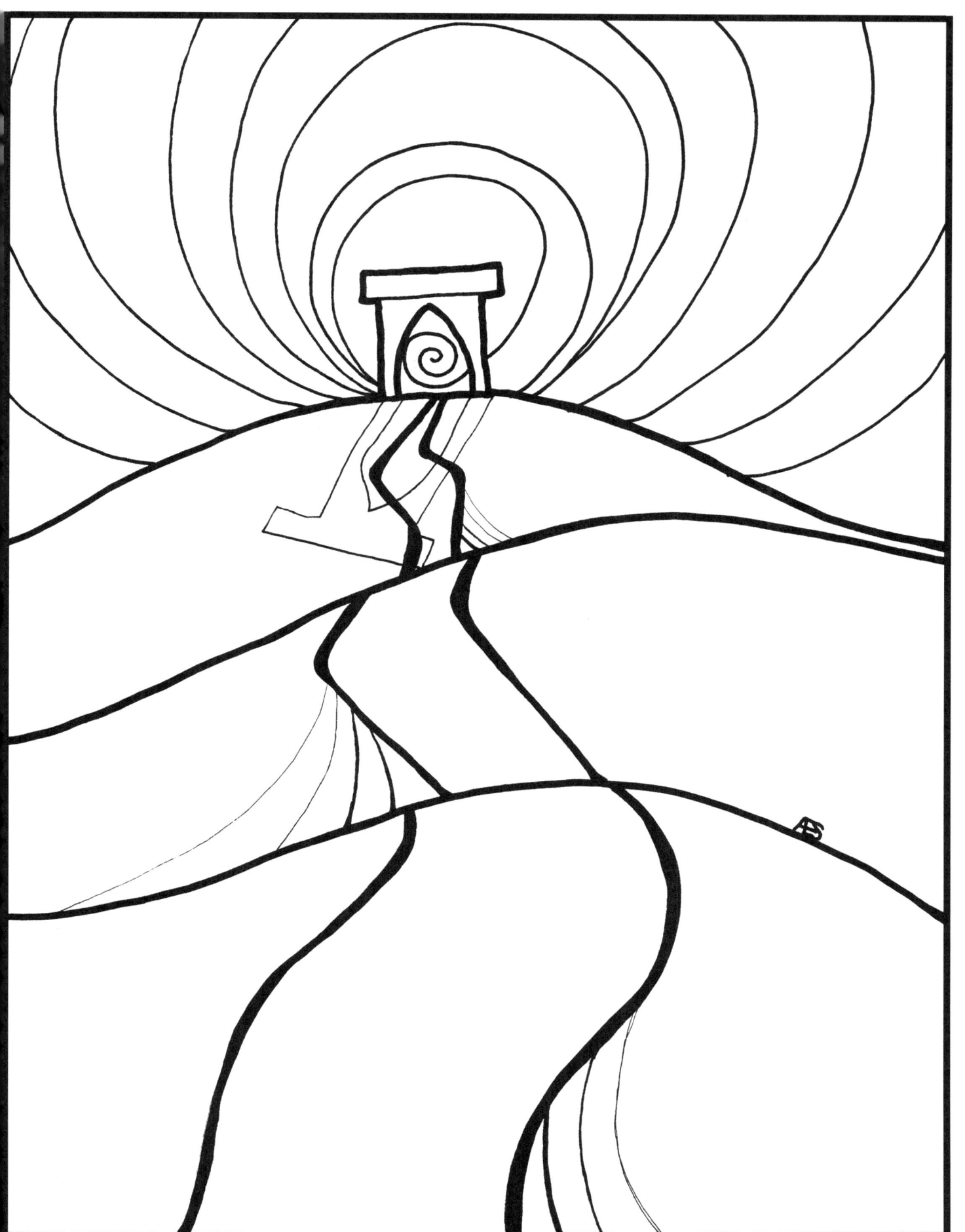

Journey's End by Annie Swarm Guldberg

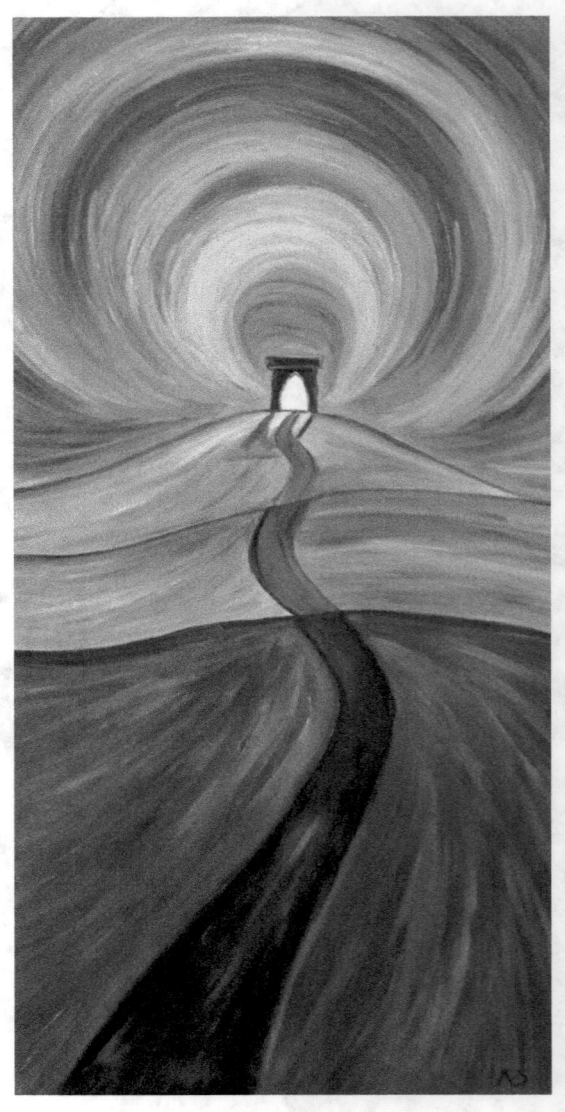

JOURNEY'S END BY ANNIE SWARM GULDBERG

The end of the journey — or is it just the beginning?
The only way to find out is to go on in.

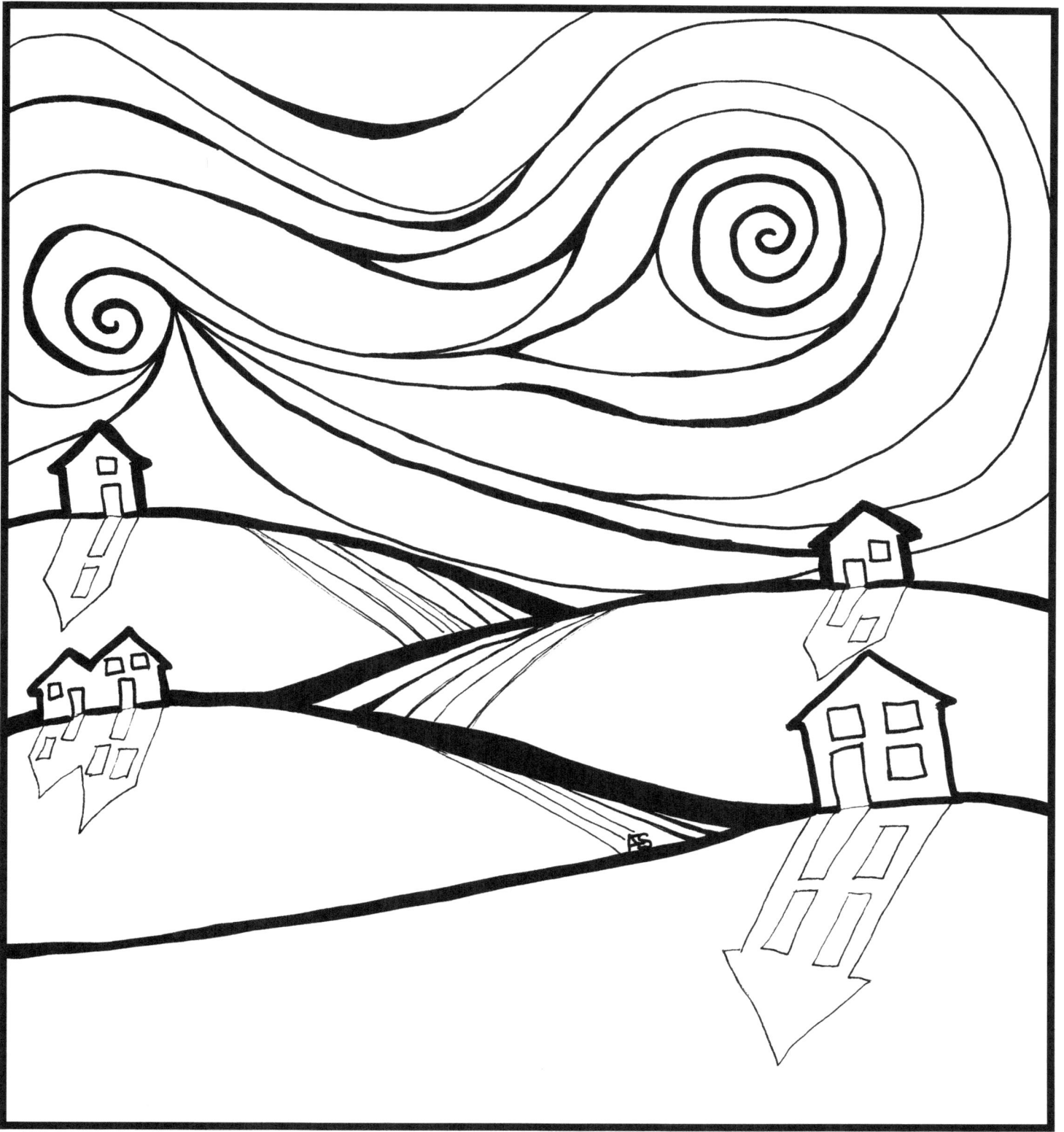

Paper Houses by Annie Swarm Guldberg

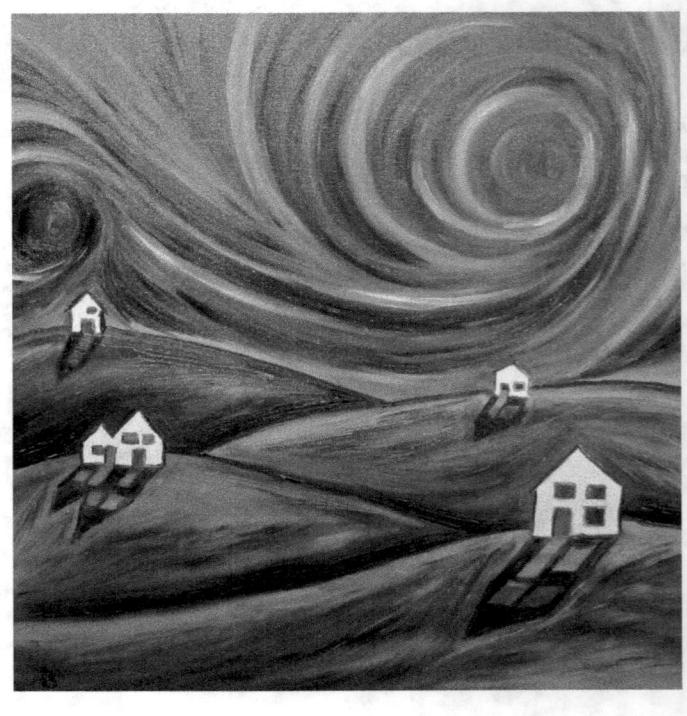

PAPER HOUSES BY ANNIE SWARM GULDBERG

Inspired by the contrast of sky, land, and
homes while driving through Iowa.

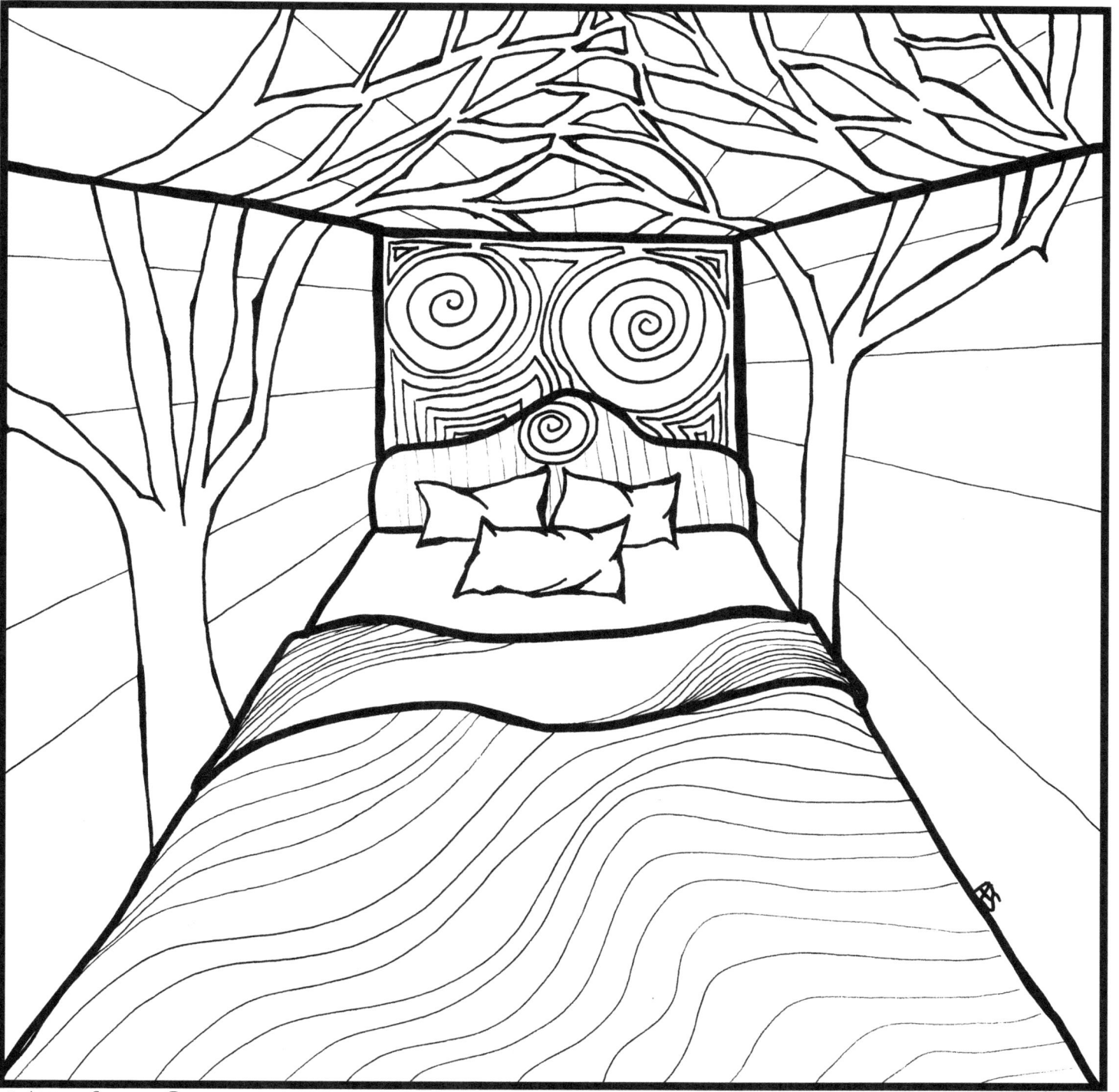

Getaway by Annie Swarm Guldberg

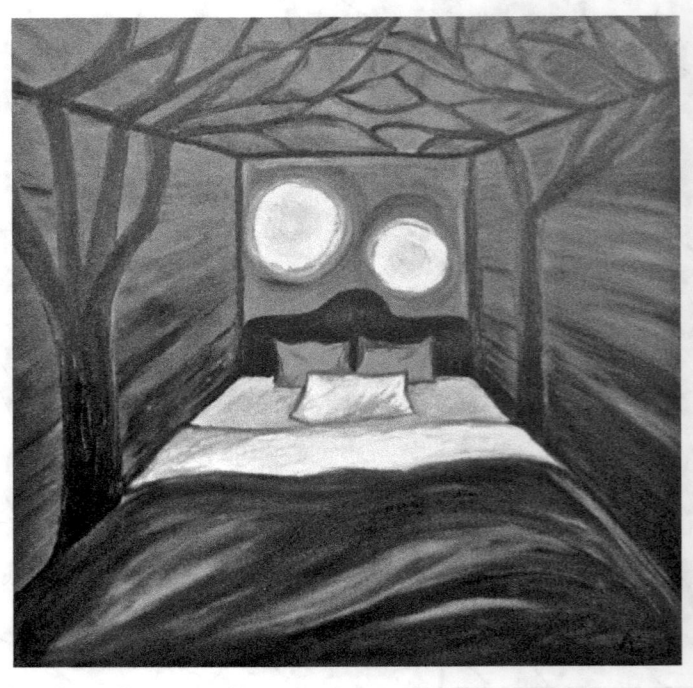

GETAWAY BY ANNIE SWARM GULDBERG

We all need a little getaway from time to time.
What better way to escape than in your own dreams?

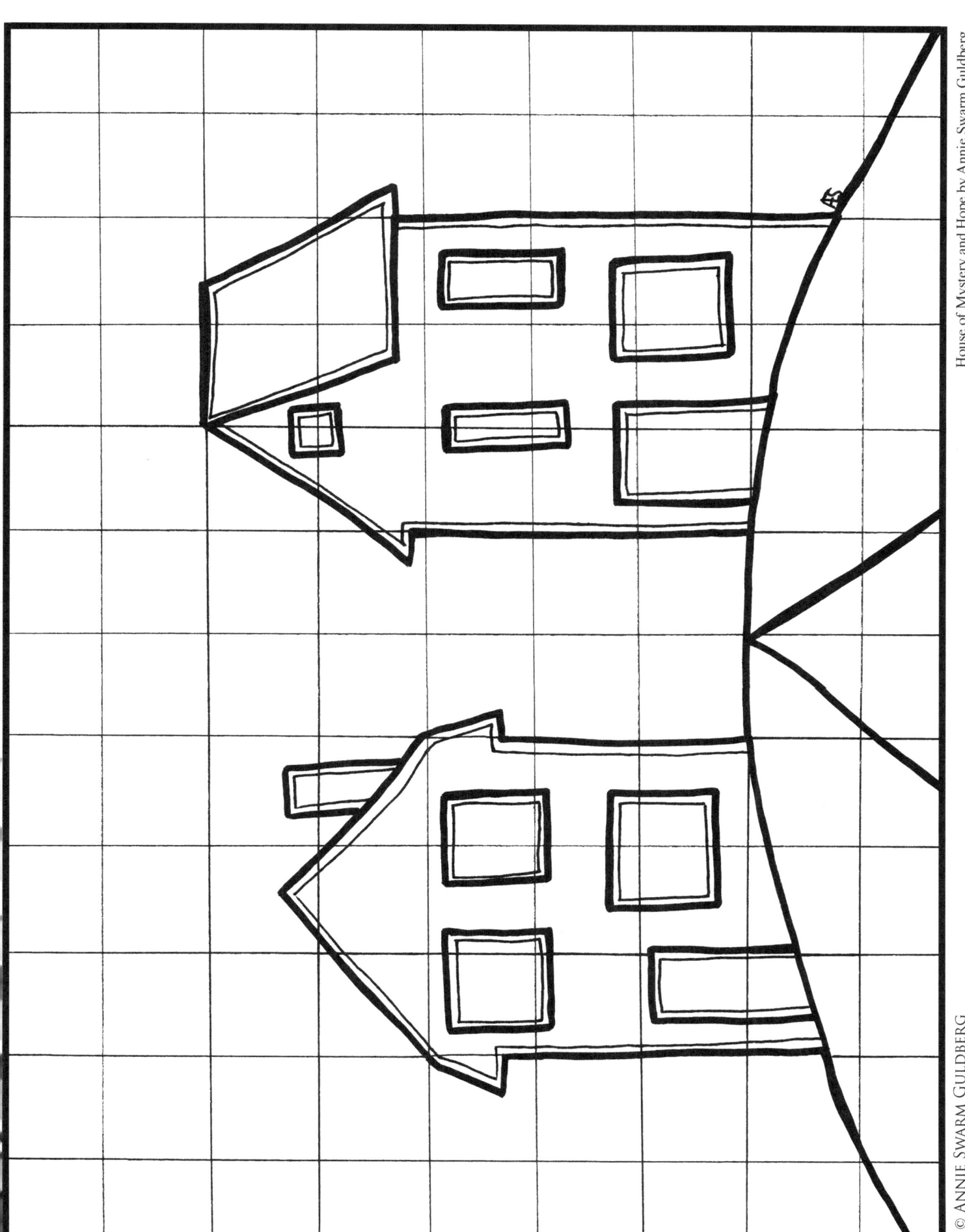

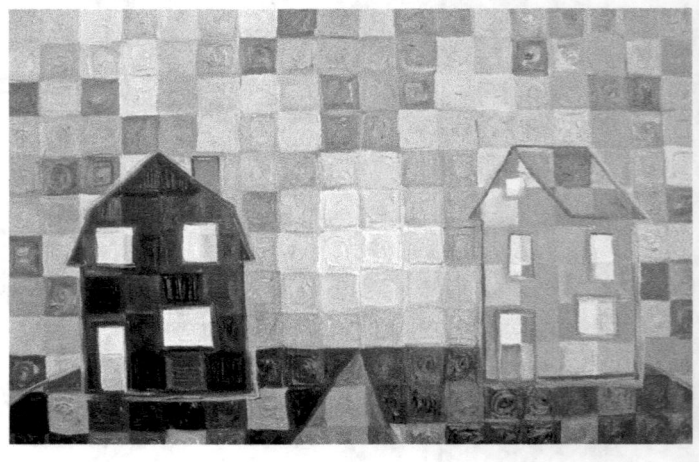

HOUSE OF MYSTERY AND HOPE
BY ANNIE SWARM GULDBERG

With a path going between the two, we see the
division and difference between mystery and hope —
though they are very close neighbors.

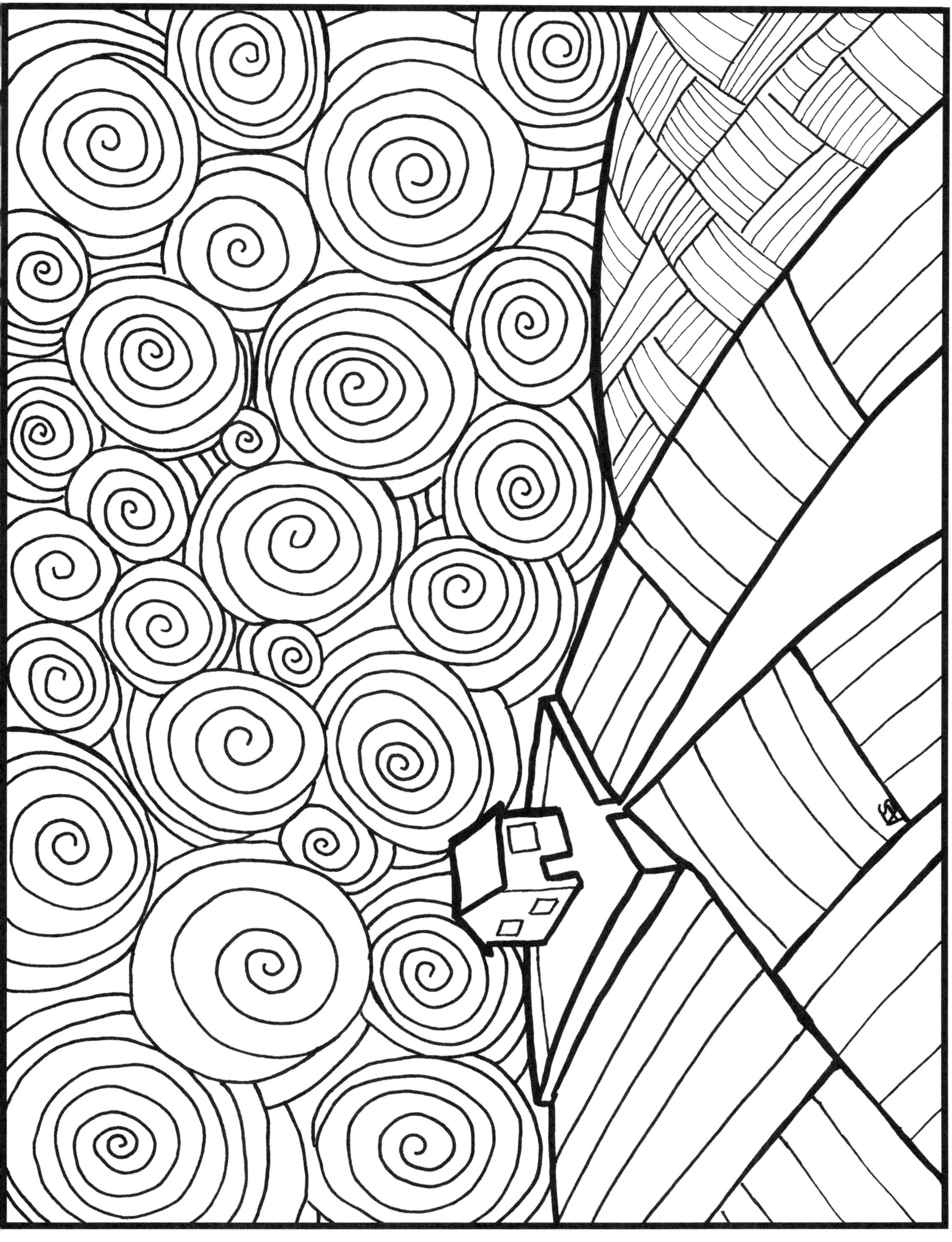

Growing Season by Annie Swarm Guldberg

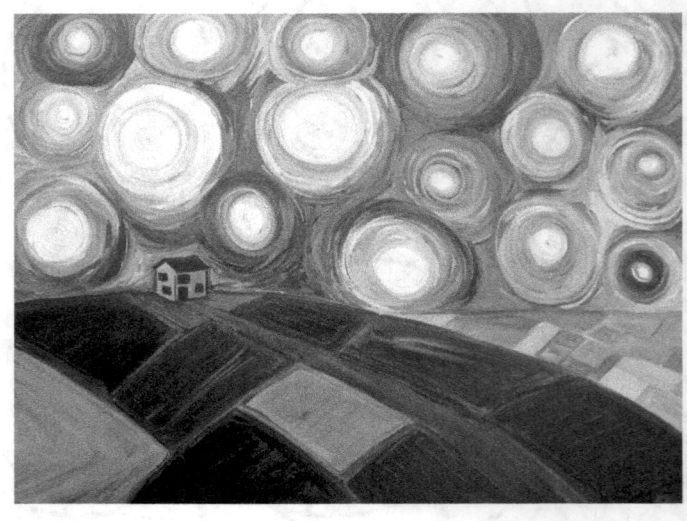

GROWING SEASON BY ANNIE SWARM GULDBERG

Inspired by the fields of Iowa in the height of summer —
everything is growing, and the sky is exploding
with color and possibilities.

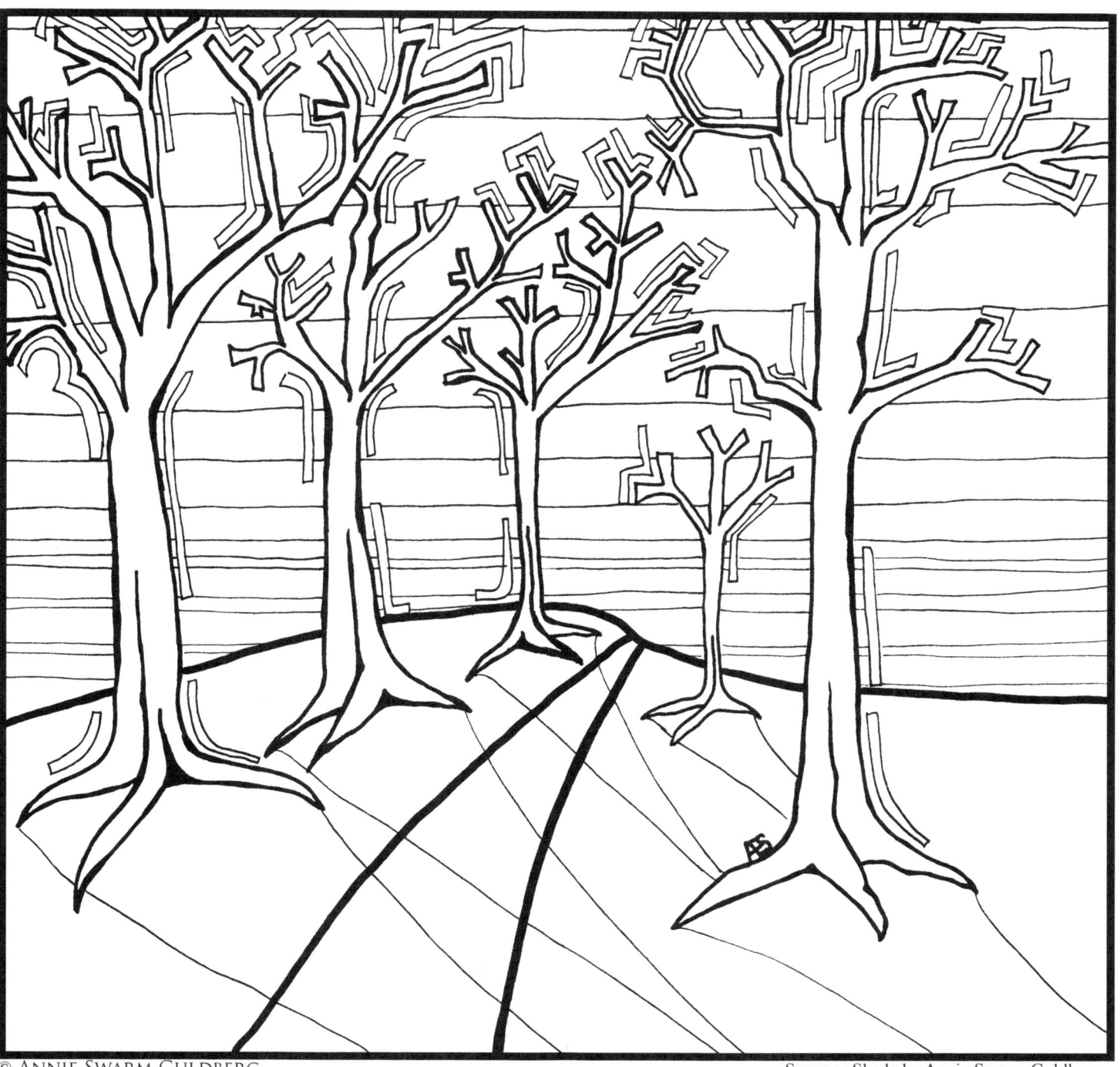

Summer Shade by Annie Swarm Guldberg

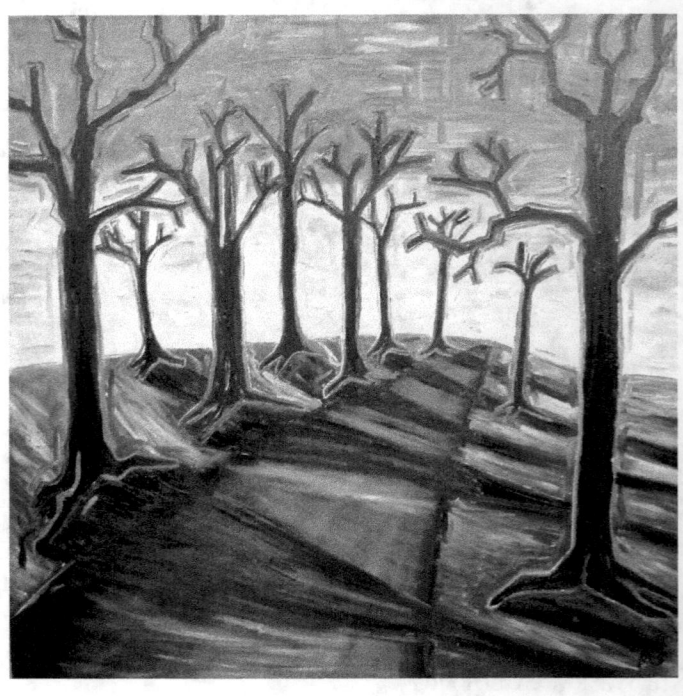

SUMMER SHADE BY ANNIE SWARM GULDBERG

Inspired by the soft summer light and shadows.

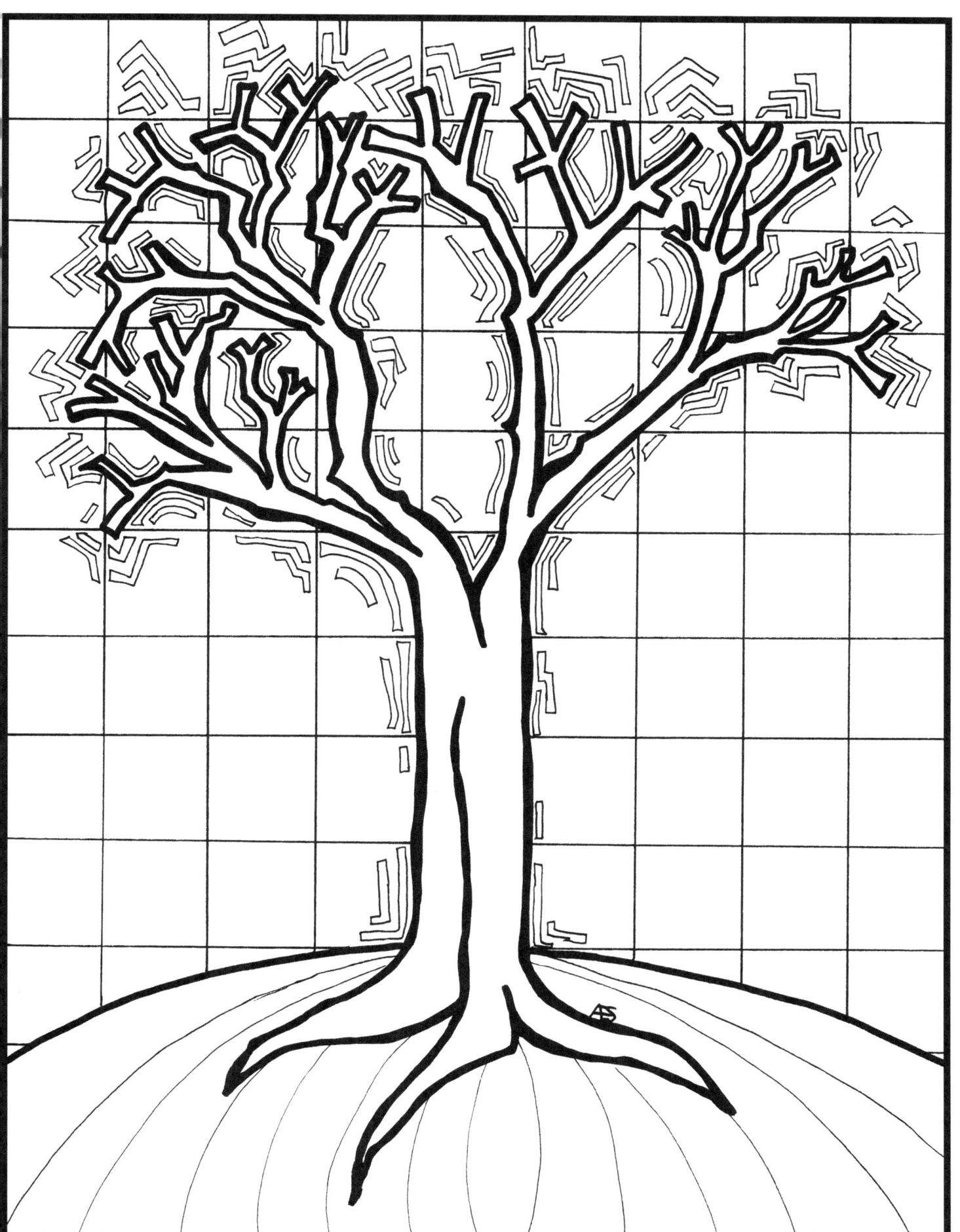

Powers of Recall by Annie Swarm Guldberg

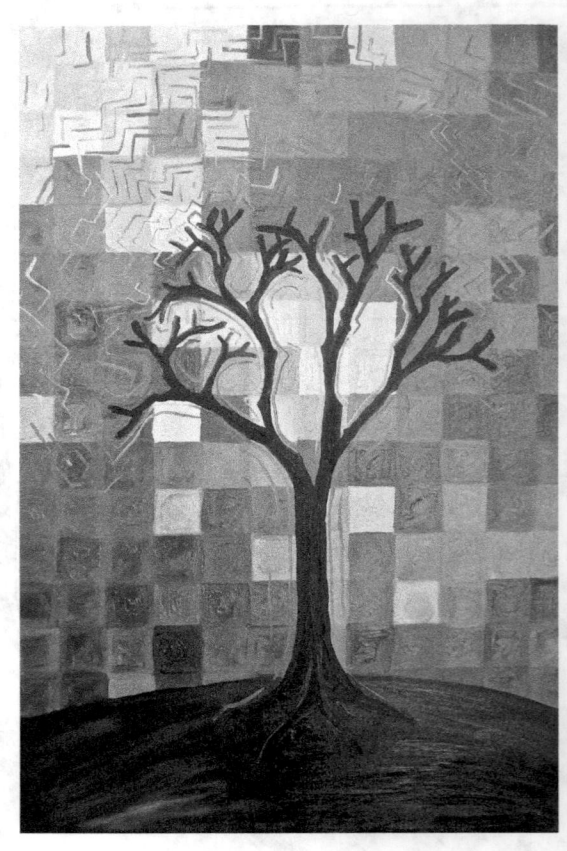

POWERS OF RECALL BY ANNIE SWARM GULDBERG

This painting is about the rich histories we all have —
friendships, experiences, joys and tragedies, and the importance
of remembering how they all make us who we are.

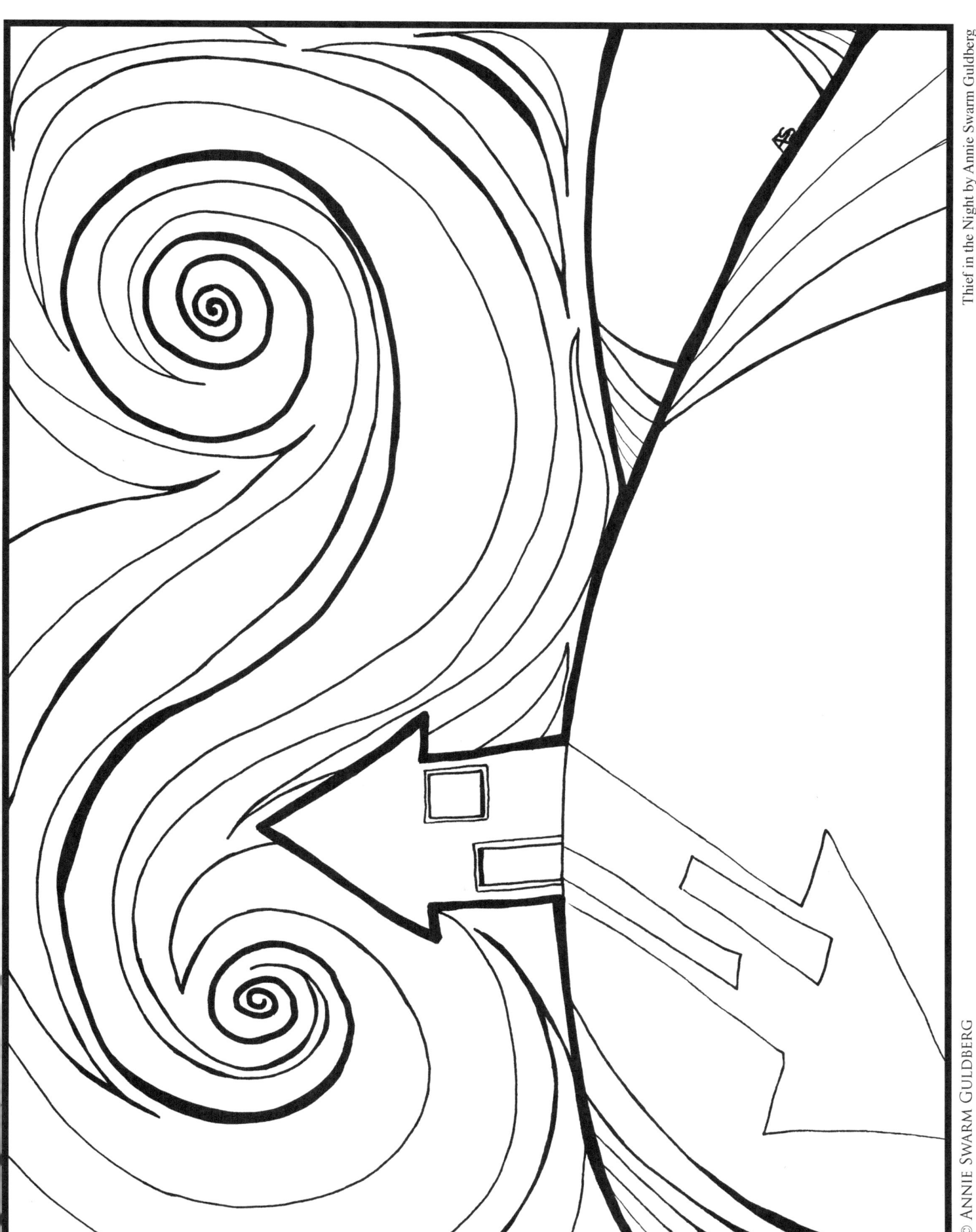

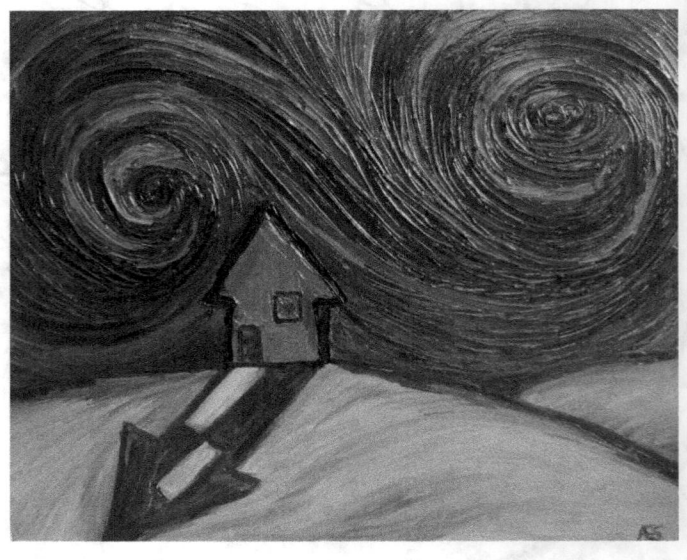

THIEF IN THE NIGHT BY ANNIE SWARM GULDBERG

The title of this painting comes from the ominous swirl in the
sky, and the emptiness of the house — both in the door and
window, and in the haunting shadow.

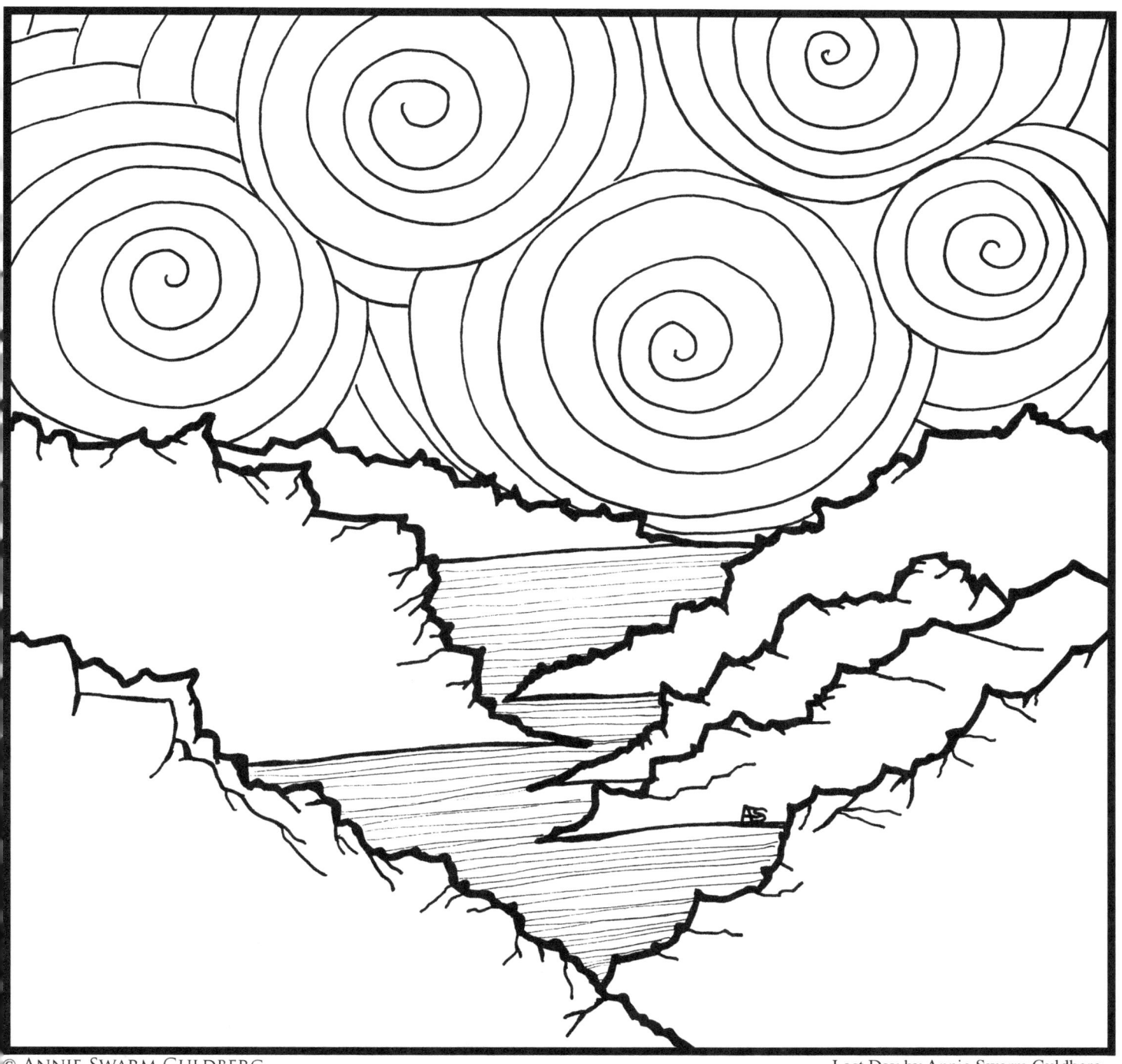

Last Day by Annie Swarm Guldberg

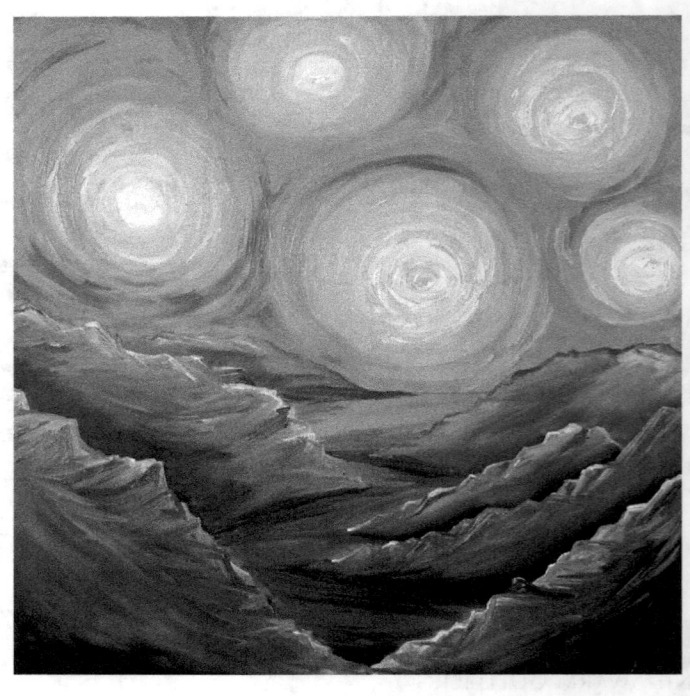

LAST DAY BY ANNIE SWARM GULDBERG

My interpretation of the last day on earth.
Either the end of the world, or your
own last day as you fly away.